# Getting a Job

**Leanne Currie-McGhee**

San Diego, CA

**About the Author**

Leanne Currie-McGhee has been writing for nearly two decades and loves her job. She lives in Norfolk, Virginia, with her husband, Keith, and their daughters, Grace and Hope.

© 2020 ReferencePoint Press, Inc.
Printed in the United States

For more information, contact:
ReferencePoint Press, Inc.
PO Box 27779
San Diego, CA 92198
www.ReferencePointPress.com

Picture Credits:
Cover: Andrey_Popov/Shutterstock.com
  5: Minerva Studio/Shutterstock.com
  9: Stokkete/Shutterstock.com
12: michaeljung/Depositphotos
16: Brad Ingram/Shutterstock.com
19: Shutterstock.com
24: Monkey Business Images/Shutterstock.com
27: dennizn/Shutterstock.com
32: fizkes/Shutterstock.com
35: Monkey Business Images/Shutterstock.com
39: Andrey_Popov/Shutterstock.com
41: pixelheadphoto digitalskillet/Shutterstock.com
46: Maksym Azovtsev/Shutterstock.com
48: inLite Studio/Shutterstock.com
54: Monkey Business Images/Shutterstock.com

LIBRARY OF CONGRESS CATALOGING-IN-PUBLICATION DATA

Name: Currie-McGhee, L.K. (Leanne K.), author.
Title: Getting a Job/By Leanne Currie-McGhee.
Description: San Diego, CA: ReferencePoint Press, Inc., [2019] | Series: Teen Life Skills | Includes
    bibliographical references and index. | Audience: Grade 9 to 12.
Identifiers: LCCN 2019003446 (print) | LCCN 2019015396 (ebook) | ISBN 9781682827444
    (eBook) | ISBN 9781682827437 (hardback) Subjects: LCSH: Job hunting—Juvenile literature. |
    Vocational guidance—Juvenile literature.
Classification: LCC HF5382.7 (ebook) | LCC HF5382.7 .C88 2019 (print) | DDC 650.14—dc23
LC record available at https://lccn.loc.gov/2019003446

# CONTENTS

# Different Jobs at Different Stages

Most people will have to get a job at some point in their lives, and most will continue working for many years. In October 2018, according to the Bureau of Labor Statistics, 129.63 million people worked full time (thirty-five hours or more a week) in the United States, and 27.33 million worked part time (less than thirty-five hours per week). This equates to approximately 48 percent of the entire US population and 75 percent of the working-age population (aged fifteen to sixty-four).

Why do people work? The short answer is simple—to make money. People need money to purchase necessities, including food, shelter, and clothing. People also want money to spend on nonessential but enjoyable pursuits, such as entertainment and travel. Others may work for more specific goals, such as funding their education or saving up for a car. Men and women also work to take care of their families as well as themselves. Martha Artyomenko, currently working as a property manager, remembers the exact reason she got her first job. "I got my driver's license at the age of 16. Along with having my driver's license, my parents' car insurance doubled," Artyomenko recalls. "As a sort of rite of passage, I took on my own expenses, which were not a lot at that point, but I got a part time job at the local library to pay for car insurance, gas expenses, clothing and save some of the rest."[1]

Though money may be the ultimate driving force behind getting a job, many other factors play into the type of job a person seeks. Some may choose professions in which they feel they are making a positive difference in the world, such as becoming a doctor or a minister. Others may enter a career because they are skilled in a certain area, such as cooking or welding, and want to use this skill. People also may be drawn to a job because they know someone they admire in that career, such as joining the military if a parent or older sibling served. Working at a job that suits a person well often leads to greater satisfaction with both the job and life.

## Teens Who Work

At age sixteen Leah worked five hours a day, four to five days a week, at J. Christopher's, a chain restaurant, because she wanted

A primary reason people work is to make money. They need money for a variety of things including food, clothes, rent, education, entertainment, and travel.

to be more independent. "I don't want to depend on anyone else for my money," Leah explains. "I want to work for myself, and earn my stuff, myself."[2] She paid for her own gas, her monthly cell phone bill, and her clothes with her own money while still attending school. Leah is one of the millions of teens who help make up the workforce. While the majority of American workers are aged twenty-five to fifty-four years, millions of others are teenagers. According to the Bureau of Labor Statistics, in 2017 nearly 17 million teens aged sixteen to nineteen worked at some type of job.

Teens work for different reasons. The most common reason is to earn extra money for items like entertainment and gas, while their parents continue to pay for major items like housing and food. Other teens work because they are saving for long-term goals, such as attending college or opening their own business. Still others may need jobs because they are living on their own and must pay for their housing, utilities, and all other expenses. These teens depend on the wages from their jobs to survive independently.

## The Process

No matter what their age or why they are seeking employment, most people are not excited about the actual process of finding a job. The idea of preparing a résumé, identifying potential employers, and interviewing can seem daunting to people both young and old. However, following the expertise of and tips from others can make the process smoother and less stressful. Vicki Salemi, a career expert with Monster, a job search website, gives advice on how to deal with feeling overwhelmed. "Tackle this emotion by approaching your job search like it's an actual job," Salemi writes. "Be disciplined, stay focused and take it seriously."[3]

# CHAPTER ONE

# What Kind of Work Should I Do?

Eric Pait could not have been happier. Not only had he graduated from college, he was also one of the few graduating students who had been offered an actual job—as a front-end web developer—instead of simply an unpaid internship, which is more common. Soon after graduation, Pait dove into his job with enthusiasm. As days, then weeks, passed, however, his enthusiasm quickly waned. He realized he had made the wrong choice. "It was all pretty much menial grunt work,"[4] he says of his job, explaining that it was not at all what he expected. Six months later, he quit.

Pait learned that you should not take a job simply because it is offered. Whether they work part time or full time, people spend hours at their jobs, and no one wants to spend those hours performing tasks they dislike or having to tolerate a negative work environment. This situation is, however, not uncommon. According to a survey of more than ten thousand tech employees by workplace-gossip site Blind, almost one out of four people are unhappy with their job.

That could be you, but it does not have to be. You can do your research, gain an idea of what you want to do, and determine what you are qualified for before you ever begin your job search. Experts suggest this will make the job search less stressful and

# Understanding Job Restrictions

Getting a job is a major step for teens who want to take a step toward independence. However, you might not be able to work as many hours as you want or at the type of job you want, because of your age. In the United States the Fair Labor Standards Act sets the minimum age for employment at fourteen. It also limits the number of hours minors who are under age sixteen can work, and it prohibits the employment of a minor in work declared hazardous by the US secretary of labor. This hazardous work includes excavation, driving, and the operation of many types of power-driven equipment. States may also have specific laws that are stricter than the Fair Labor Standards Act. Because of this, it is important for teens to know whether there are any restrictions that might limit the types of jobs for which they can apply.

more likely to result in a satisfying job that is compatible with your interests and abilities.

## What Do You Like?

The first step in a job search is to determine what your interests are. Begin by making a list of your hobbies, extracurricular and/or volunteer activities, and any previous jobs that you have enjoyed. This will help you recognize the areas that interest you most. For example, walking dogs and volunteering with the American Society for the Prevention of Cruelty to Animals (ASPCA) show an interest in working with animals, while watching kids during church services or babysitting for neighbors indicates you enjoy working with children.

Another way to zero in on your strengths and interests is to take online quizzes specifically developed by organizations with a background in career matching. For example, the Princeton Career Quiz asks questions to determine what types of jobs a person might find interesting. The questions cover areas such as whether someone prefers to accept the asking price or bargain for a better price when buying an item such as a car and whether one prefers to be moving while doing work or sitting still and concentrating. The answers to questions like these help identify the kinds of careers and jobs most likely to fit one's personality.

## Skills Needed

While it is important to know what you are interested in doing, it is equally important to be realistic about the job skills you have to offer. Understanding what your skills are and working to develop additional ones will increase your chances of finding a job. These skills can be hard skills, which are technical and measurable, such as being able to program in a specific computer language or fluently speak another language such as Spanish. Skills can also be soft, such as the ability to listen and communicate effectively, be a good motivator, or learn new tasks quickly.

As with interests, making a list of skills will help guide a person starting a job search. When considering what hard and soft skills

*According to a study of ten thousand tech employees, almost one in four people is unhappy with their job. Experts stress doing your research before applying for and accepting a job.*

you have, you should take into account all the different areas of your life, from school to clubs. Your skill set can include skills from classes that you excel in, such as knowing how to use Linux from a computer class. Other skills may have been obtained from activities, such as learning to write clearly while working on a school newspaper as a student reporter. Leadership and communication skills may be developed in pursuits such as being an organizer of a food drive or participating in a debate club. Additionally, if you have any work experience, you should list the skills learned at prior jobs. This list of skills will help you identify your strengths and interests and how these can transfer to a job.

## Why I Want a Job

The most important factor is to understand why you are searching for a job. Whether searching for your first job or wanting to leave a current job for a new one, understanding your reasons for

## Building Up Skills

What if you don't have many skills that could help you get a job? Ayn Bernos suggests acquiring additional skills and claims that it is not difficult to do. Bernos, a freelance writer and marketing specialist, explains that before she started her job search, she made sure she developed skills related to her field, such as knowing how to write a press release and how to create a presentation. "If you don't have any skills right now, then, work on it," she advises. "You can research and acquire skills. Google 'how to Photoshop' or 'how to write an essay,' or 'how to write an article.' Google different areas and then actually learn them, to add to your resume." By expanding her skills, Bernos was able to find a job in her desired field.

Ayn Bernos, "How to Make a CV/Resume," YouTube, November 10, 2017. www.youtube .com/watch?v=tUwoX6N_AZE.

doing so will point you in the right direction during your search.

Although money is often the driving force for a seeking a job, there can be other reasons as well, such as determining what you want to do for a long-term career. Alyssa, for example, viewed her first job as a way to determine if she wanted to work with dogs as a career. She grew up loving dogs and decided to follow that interest as she entered the workforce. At age nineteen she was hired as a veterinary assistant at a veterinary clinic. Over the two and a half years that she worked there, her interest in and knowledge about dog behavior continued to expand. Her next job was as a dog care attendant at a dog day care, and then she moved on to a job at Petco, where she attended a dog trainer program. "To put it simply," says Alyssa, "I am crazy about dogs. For as long as I can remember, I have felt a deep connection to these wonderful creatures."[5] Today, she offers dog training and behavior services and is co-owner of a dog day care program, where owners can drop off their dogs to be watched during the day. She views her first job as the start to a satisfying career path.

> "I am crazy about dogs. For as long as I can remember, I have felt a deep connection to these wonderful creatures."[5]
>
> —Alyssa, co-owner of a dog day care

Others may be looking for a job that will give them experience in a career field they are interested in pursuing. For example, a person might dream of being a video game designer, but to get a foot in the door, he or she could take a job as a game tester. This job is in the same industry but does not require as much experience as a designer. Though this may not be the person's ideal job, it nonetheless provides experience and a foothold in the field.

## Job Types

One more key point to remember before you start your search is to be realistic about the kind of job you can get. Typically, a teenager will have little or no work background. While there are instances of young adults becoming rich after they have become

The ability to communicate effectively is considered a soft skill. Understanding what your skills are and working to develop new ones will increase your chances of finding a job you will be satisfied with.

a YouTube sensation or developed a great new technology application or product, these happenings are rare. To move up in a career, both in terms of position and money, you need to gain job skills. To start, someone with few skills can seek entry-level jobs such as working as a cashier at a store or as a food service worker in a fast-food restaurant.

The level of job a person is qualified for affects the type of pay he or she will receive. Generally, entry-level jobs pay by the hour, and the pay is minimum wage. The federal minimum wage was $7.25 in 2018, although some cities and states have set higher minimum wages. Jobs that require greater skills and experience typically are more highly paid and may be salaried jobs, which means a person earns a specific annual wage no matter how many hours he or she works.

A realistic assessment of your personal interests, skills, experience, and reasons for wanting a job, as well as factors such as time availability and access to transportation, will enable you to determine what kind of job to search for and what pay level you can expect. Rahul Patle moved to the United States from India to study computer science. When he obtained his master's degree, he considered his skills and interests and where he wanted to live. "While I was in college, my pet projects taught me about my strengths and weaknesses, and I discovered my passion for converting ideas into real products," Patle explains. "During my job search, I'd decided to only seek opportunities in the [San Francisco] Bay Area because that was where innovative things seemed to be happening."[6] After an extensive search, Patle came across an opening for a job as a user experience engineer for a company that produces apps. He applied for the job and was hired. Today he is engaged in and excited by his job.

> "While I was in college, my pet projects taught me about my strengths and weaknesses, and I discovered my passion for converting ideas into real products."[6]
>
> —Rahul Patle, user experience engineer

With persistence and effort, you can have a result like Patle's. If you dedicate yourself to carefully considering what you want to do and what you are capable of doing before the job search, your eventual result just might be a satisfying job.

# CHAPTER TWO

# Résumé Rules

Ben was ready to get a job. He knew he wanted to work in the web-development field. Although he did not have a degree in the field or work experience in it, he acquired skills by attending a boot camp to learn JavaScript, HTML, and other web languages. He also developed websites on his own to add to his accomplishments. Then he needed a résumé. Ben researched and determined how best to display his skills on a résumé, highlighting what he did know about technology despite his lack of a degree in the field. "If you've done personal projects, just list personal projects and the technology used,"[7] he says he was advised. That is what Ben did. He also included a link to a website that gave more detail on those projects. After doing this, Ben began sending his resume to IT companies and they responded. Ben's approach worked, and he soon was hired for his first job as a web developer.

Ben's résumé was effective because he understood that a résumé is an essential tool needed to express who an applicant is and why a company should hire him or her. A résumé describes your education, job experience (if any), your skills and how you acquired them, and any other relevant information about you that relates to the type of job you want. The key to a good résumé is to be honest and forthright about your strengths and skills.

"You have only a few seconds to snag the employer's attention,"[8] writes Seattle-based career coach Robin Ryan. For that reason, your résumé needs to be succinct and interesting.

## List, Then Write

A good first step in composing a résumé is to create a list of your relevant education, experience, and skills. For first-time job seekers, education is typically the most important section. Include the schools you have attended and any honors you have received. For a high school student, this could include being named to the honor roll, whereas a college graduate could list that he or she graduated cum laude (with honors). Include any extracurricular activites you took part in. If you have work experience, list all the jobs you have had and write brief descriptions of your duties in each. Include volunteer experience as well, particularly if you obtained specific skills as a volunteer—such as leading a project, working with animals, or building a website. Lastly, list any relevant skills, such as knowing how to program in C+, being fluent in another language such as Spanish or Chinese, or being certified or licensed in something that is relevant to the job.

"You have only a few seconds to snag the employer's attention."[8]

—Robin Ryan, career coach

Once you have finished your list of accomplishments and skills, you are ready to compose the résumé. Software applications such as Microsoft Word have résumé templates that you can use, or you can download a free template from a résumé website. A template is already formatted, so all you have to do is enter your information in the appropriate fields.

At the top you will enter basic information about yourself—your name, telephone number, and email address. Ensure that the email address is professional instead of something like partywithjill@msn.com that will create a poor impression of you. Next is usually the heading "Objective," under which you enter your job goal. Examples of an objective statement are "Seeking a position as a responsible child-care worker," "Outdoor lover

For first-time job seekers, education is typically the most important section on a résumé. Be sure to include the schools you have attended and any honors you have received.

seeking a job as a camp counselor," and "Journalism graduate seeking an entry-level position in a publishing company." Your goal should be clear and concise.

Following this, a résumé typically contains information about work experience, skills, and education. The order of these sections depends on which attributes you want to highlight most. For example, those with more work experience would put this information first. Under the heading "Experience," list all the jobs you have had and provide descriptions of the main duties you performed at each. Include any volunteer positions relevant to the job you are seeking as well. For those with little or no job experience, listing skills or education first may work better to highlight your strengths.

## Accurate and Concise

Once you have completed your résumé, reread it carefully. It is of utmost importance that it be accurate, including not stretching the truth or outright lying about your qualifications. Lying may get you to an interview, but it is ethically wrong and will almost always be found out. One recruiter recalls confronting an applicant with a lie. "I looked at a candidate's resume and LinkedIn profile right before an interview and noticed his resume indicated that he had a degree while his LinkedIn profile did not," the recruiter recalls. "When I asked him point-blank if he had received his degree, he admitted that he had not done so."[9] The applicant did not get the job.

In addition to providing accurate information, it is essential to eliminate any grammar or spelling errors. A résumé is your first opportunity to make a good impression, and errors convey the

### Learning from Mistakes

Andy Sterkowitz landed his first programming job without any experience in that field and only a small amount of related schooling. He attributes getting his foot in the door to his résumé—but not the first version of it. He used that version to apply to twenty-seven companies; only four responded at all, and those four rejected him. His major problem was that the work history he provided, such as being a law clerk, had nothing to do with being a programmer.

For his next version, he decided to be more creative. Instead of job experience, he focused the résumé on what the software apps that he created do and how he coded them. He also used powerful statements like "Software development is an engaging challenge." The result—he got an interview and his first programming job. "The big takeaway is," he says, "if . . . you are using one approach to a resume and it's not working—be willing to try different things and be willing to get creative."

Andy Sterkowitz, "Resume That Landed My First Job," YouTube, May 8, 2018. www.youtube.com/watch?v=Mi8bptpUqto.

impression that you are sloppy or careless. A bad first impression usually leads to immediate rejection. It is a good idea to have a friend or relative review your résumé to catch any errors you may have overlooked.

Keeping the résumé brief is a must because recruiters have many to review. One page is typically enough for a person with ten or fewer years of experience. A good way to draw the attention of the reviewer in such a brief document is to use short, direct action words. For those lacking much experience, using adjectives can help express your excitement about and commitment to a job. "On recent graduate resumes, adjectives I like to include are 'energetic,' 'enthusiastic,' or 'persistent,'" says Michelle Robin, chief career brand officer at Brand Your Career. "Since recent graduates don't often have a ton of experience, it is important to demonstrate how they have the right spirit to attack challenges they may come across in the workplace."[10]

"On recent graduate resumes, adjectives I like to include are 'energetic,' 'enthusiastic,' or 'persistent.'"[10]

—Michelle Robin, chief career brand officer

## Cover Letter

Once your résumé is finished, you are still not quite ready to submit it to prospective employers. There is one remaining task. Recruiters advise that applicants include a cover letter with any résumé, whether submitted electronically or on paper. A cover letter is a way of introducing yourself to the recruiter or company hiring manager.

As with résumés, there are many cover letter templates available online at websites such as Zety. A template will include places to enter the name and address of the company to which you are applying, your name and contact info, a greeting, two to three paragraphs for the letter's body, and a closing with room for your signature. Keep the body paragraphs of the letter short and professional. The first should state who you are, such as a

Keeping the résumé brief is a must because recruiters have many résumés to review. One page is typically enough for a person with ten or fewer years of experience.

RESUME

## Limited Time

The reason prospective employees need to make their résumé interesting is they have little time to catch a hiring manager's attention. According to a survey on CareerBuilder, an estimated 40 percent of hiring managers spend less than sixty seconds reviewing each résumé they receive—and 25 percent spend less than thirty seconds. Because of this, highlight your major accomplishments in such a way that they are easy to spot and read. Additionally, avoid hard-to-read fonts and overuse of formatting such as italics and boldface, so that your résumé is uncluttered and visually appealing.

college student studying engineering or an outgoing high school student interested in customer service; the opportunity you are interested in; and how you found out about that opportunity. The second paragraph outlines the skills or characteristics you have that qualify you for the job. As an example, if you were applying for a child care position, you would include past babysitting jobs or first aid courses you have taken. The last paragraph should thank the company for considering you and include a sentence stating that your résumé is attached.

## The Need for a Portfolio

For most people a résumé and a cover letter are all that is needed to apply for a job. But those who are seeking certain jobs, such as graphic artists, photographers, and writers, may also need to include a portfolio. A portfolio is a compilation of samples of work in a specific area. For example, a person applying to work as a graphic artist for a video game company will likely need to show his or her previous work and style with a portfolio. An ideal way to do this is to create a website where the best works are showcased with applicable information, such as the video game name and when it was produced.

Leslie Kirchhoff's portfolio landed her a dream job. While attending New York University, Kirchhoff accepted an internship at *Vogue* magazine to work on its website. While there, she asked her bosses to look at her photography portfolio, which included fashion photographs that she had taken on her own time. Her bosses were impressed and assigned her a celebrity party to photograph. This led to additional assignments photographing well-known fashion events and personalities. "I quickly became one of their go-to photographers for the website, shooting everything from parties to runway shows to portraits and more,"[11] states Kirchhoff. She continued working for *Vogue* as a freelancer, and today, in her twenties, she has become a well-known fashion photographer.

A résumé and portfolio can open the door to almost any job. They are the first look a potential employer has at you and what you have to offer in a workplace. That is why putting your best self on paper is an essential step in your job search.

# CHAPTER THREE

# Networking

Jae Lee got an interview and subsequently a job because of a T-shirt. It was not the T-shirt itself, but the fact that she wore it to an event where she met people in her prospective career field, information technology. The keynote speaker from IBM, after giving a lecture, noticed the shirt, which stated "Open Source: In a world without walls, who needs Gates?," and stopped her to ask about Linux, an open source operating system. After chatting, he took down her name and phone number and said he'd be in touch. "2 months later, I got a call to go interview for an internship with Freightliner's AIX group. After the interview, I was offered a job,"[12] Lee recalls. Her internship led to a position as a systems programmer just three months later. Lee's networking, through which she met and connected with the speaker and others at the event, resulted in a job she loves.

Networking is the simple act of meeting people and establishing relationships. These connections can positively impact your chances of getting an interview and subsequently a job. According to a LinkedIn report, 70 percent of people in 2016 were hired at a company where they had a connection to another person. With so much competition in the job market, it helps to have a personal link that can help you get a foot in the door of a company.

## How to Network

One way to network is simply by letting people know that you are searching for a job and describing the types of jobs you are interested in. This is as easy as talking to friends, friends' parents, coaches, teachers, almost anyone you are in contact with—all of these interactions are a part of networking. The people you talk to can tell you whether they know of any companies that are hiring or tell you about companies that they like and recommend you learn more about. David Carlson credits networking for almost every job he has ever held, from his current one as an accountant

## Getting a Job Through Instagram

Networking through social media landed Nicola Easterby a job even though she was not looking for one. This sort of thing doesn't happen very often. But Easterby's experience does show how social media can increase visibility—which can be helpful when looking for a job. Easterby took a year off from college to travel around the world. A photography major, she decided to post her pictures on Instagram, a social media site for sharing photos, so her connections could see and enjoy her work. Topdeck Travel, a travel agency, noticed the pictures and reached out to her. As a result, the agency hired her to take pictures of her travels, which it used in its brochures. This led to her decision to work full time as a photograper for Topdeck Travel and other clients. "Five years after leaving school, I might not have a university degree, the high-paying job, a husband or a house with a white picket fence," writes Easterby. "Instead, I'm at sitting at my office, which today is a cafe by a beach at Goa, in India. As I stare past my laptop screen to sun setting beneath the waves, aromatic spices waft through the air and a salty breeze tickles my face."

Nicola Easterby, "My Gap Year Turned into a Dream Career," News.com.au, 2019. www .news.com.au.

to his first job at a Pizza Hut restaurant. "I networked into [the Piz-za Hut] job because my friend worked there," Carlson explains. "He knew I was looking for a job, so he talked to the manager and soon enough I was a freshly minted Pizza Hut cook."[13]

Joining clubs or volunteering with organizations is also a meth-od of networking. Computer coding clubs, charity groups, drama clubs, and other local groups are a good way to meet others who share your interests. Let these people know that you are search-ing for a job and find out whether they know of any openings or have ideas for places you might look for a job. If you are interested in working with animals, volunteer at the zoo, aquarium, or animal shelter and network with people who work there. Teresa Goertz discovered that volunteering and joining clubs in areas related to the field she wanted to work in led to a job. After moving to

*Networking is simply the act of meeting people and establishing relationships. These connections can enhance your chances of getting an interview and subsequently a job.*

## Proven True

Gwendolyn Faraday was skeptical about networking. The idea of it made her nervous, and she doubted it would help her find work. But after teaching herself how to code, she soon realized her résumé alone could not get her a job. "I decided to take a chance and go to a Girl Develop It event," Faraday explains of going to a coding event for women. "Once I was there, I forced myself to talk to people, even if it was just to say 'Hi.' This was a turning point for me. Since taking that initial step out of my comfort zone, I've been to countless events, gotten quite a few interviews, received several offers, and have been hired twice. And all this happened in just the last year." Faraday pushed herself to attend coding and software-development events targeted to women. "Events have helped me learn a ton about current trends in coding and technology," she adds. "This knowledge has proven to be very important—both during interviews, and with projects I'm working on."

Gwendolyn Faraday, "How Going to Coding Events Helped Me Get an Awesome Job," FreeCodeCamp, May 12, 2016. https://medium.freecodecamp.org.

Seattle with her new husband, Teresa Goertz decided to change careers and become a technical writer. She started by joining the Puget Sound chapter of the Society for Technical Communication (STC), and because she had some previous background in marketing, she volunteered as the public relations chair for one of its regional conferences. After working with Goertz at the society's events, a woman from the STC hired her for a two-week trial as a contractor in a user education group at Microsoft. After the trial period ended, Goertz was hired for a permanent position.

Attending conferences about fields you are interested in is another networking option. These can range from comic book conferences to video game conferences—all depending on your interests. Bring business cards that have your name, contact information, and a brief statement about your expertise. Introduce yourself to speakers and people working vendor booths and give them a card to help them remember you.

## Be Ready

Networking in person is not always easy. Kristen McCabe admits that networking can make her feel awkward and at times nervous. But she attends events specific to her field, marketing, to meet people who could help her with her career. "Even if your brain is thinking, 'At this exact moment I am the most awkward person on earth, will a hole please open up and swallow,' take a confident stance,"[14] McCabe recommends. "Your body will make your brain follow suit. And remember to smile during conversation." McCabe recommends approaching speakers, telling them what you liked about their talk, and asking pertinent questions. When meeting others, she says to listen to what they have to say and be ready with responses about yourself.

Another piece of advice is to have an elevator speech ready whenever you have a chance to network in person. An elevator speech gets its name from the idea that it could be delivered during a brief elevator ride. It communicates who you are, what you are looking for, and how you can benefit a prospective employer. Mario Wilson works as a marketer for home repair contractors and is always looking for new clients. Much of this search occurs through networking to make his name familiar to people. He recommends that job seekers be prepared with a speech about what they have to offer and why they should be hired. "It might sound silly, but it's important to practice," Wilson explains. "When I drive to a networking meeting I bet I look pretty silly, because I look like I'm talking to myself the whole way. I'm actually rehearsing my 30-second commercial. Sometimes I rehearse in the car on the way there."[15]

> "I'm actually rehearsing my 30-second commercial. Sometimes I rehearse in the car on the way there."[15]
>
> —Mario Wilson, home repair contractor marketer, on preparing for networking

## Online Networking

Meeting people in person is not the only way to network. Social media is another way to seek job opportunities and spread information about yourself to potential employers. The most common career-related social media site is LinkedIn, a website specifically tailored to career connections. On LinkedIn people post their résumés and profiles and use them to connect to others. To start, people can use LinkedIn to connect to their email contacts, and from there, they will receive suggestions of other contacts who are in turn connected to those people. The more people who view a person's résumé and profile, the better the possibility of that person being contacted about a job.

Creating an engaging profile on LinkedIn is a way to get noticed by companies searching for candidates. To start, write a summary that includes five or six of your best accomplishments, whether they be "Developed my own app" or "Designed and

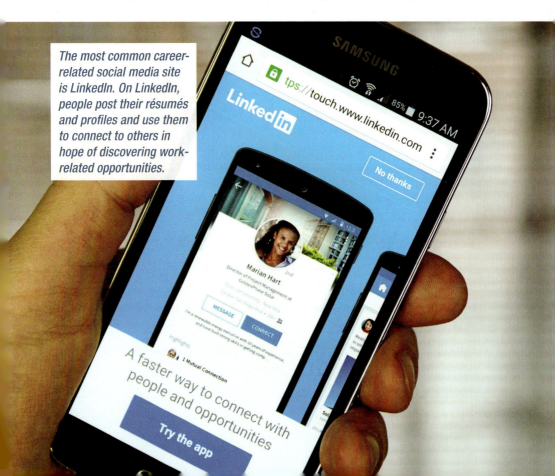

The most common career-related social media site is LinkedIn. On LinkedIn, people post their résumés and profiles and use them to connect to others in hope of discovering work-related opportunities.

fashioned my own dresses." Use forceful verbs and add pictures, if applicable. Then complete the profile, from work experience to skills to volunteer experiences, continuing to highlight your accomplishments and the skills you have obtained as a result.

Intersperse your profile with words that will attract those hiring for the types of positions you are most interested in, because recruiters search LinkedIn using keywords. When Moriah Rahamim decided she wanted to be a software engineer after years of working as a product manager, LinkedIn helped her get seven job offers in eight weeks in the field she wanted. "Recruiters use LinkedIn to find great candidates. How do they do it? The same way I search Google for Rick Astley: *'rick roll redhead 80's prank video*,'" writes Rahamim. "They use keywords, often related to the tech stack or job description, to find people with relevant experience."[16] On her LinkedIn profile, Rahamim listed all the software projects she had worked on, included all specific technologies that she had experience with, and ensured she included words like *development* and *engineer* throughout in order to pop up in searches.

LinkedIn may suggest online groups for users to join on the basis of their interests. This is also a good opportunity to expand connections. In these groups, contribute to discussions and respond to the ideas and thoughts of others. LinkedIn recommends groups based on keywords in a person's profile, but you can also search for groups. This is a way of meeting others in a meaningful way online.

## Keep Social Media Presence Clean

Whether you network in person or online, it is important to keep your social media clean because no matter how you meet people, the probability is that they will check your online presence. According to a new CareerBuilder survey, 70 percent of employers use social media to screen job candidates, which is up significantly from 60 percent in 2016. Rebecca Del Cid, a hiring manager, explains how this can affect hiring decisions. "I looked at a candidate's Facebook page and saw that he was really into music but some of his pictures were rather strange," writes Del Cid. "He would post a lot of things that were hateful and cuss a lot or would brag about his drug usage and very derogatory topics. I automatically deemed him unfit for this work environment."[17] People looking for jobs should not include cursing, pictures of themselves partying, rants or complaints about work, or anything in bad taste on any social media.

Ensuring that you show your best self during both your online and in-person interactions will open doors to opportunities. Taking the extra step to make connections with others, and letting them know who you are and what you want, can lead you to a rewarding job.

> "He would post a lot of things that were hateful and cuss a lot or would brag about his drug usage and very derogatory topics. I automatically deemed him unfit for this work environment."[17]
>
> —Rebecca Del Cid, hiring manager, on a prospective employee's social media presence

# CHAPTER FOUR

# The Search

As a junior in high school, Nicolas Cress decided it was time to get a job. He knew exactly what company he wanted to try first, after having considered his skills and interests. "The YMCA has been involved in my life since I was little. What started out as attending birthday parties for my friends at the Downtown Facilities quickly turned into years of swimming lessons when the Valley Y opened in 2000," Cress explains. "As I reached the end of my Junior Year at High School I found myself in the same predicament as most other kids my age. It was time to get a job."[18] Cress reached out to learn more about job possibilities at the YMCA. With some networking help from his brother, who was a lifeguard at another YMCA in the area, Cress learned that YMCA day camps were hiring. After an application and interview, Cress got a job as a camp counselor.

As Cress did, the best way to begin the actual job search after assessing interests, strengths, and skills; developing a résumé; and starting to network is to focus on companies you are most interested in working for at this stage of life. Begin by making a list of any companies and organizations you are aware of that you think would be a good fit. These are companies that pique your interest on the basis of your skills and likes. For example, if you want to work with animals, list organizations such as the ASPCA and companies such as Petco. If your dream job is to be surrounded by books, add nearby bookstores or libraries. Outdoor lovers may consider local, state, and national parks; camps; and gardens and other outdoor facilities. Continue to expand this list as you learn about additional organizations or companies that might have jobs meeting your expectations. Also, research what companies are competitors of those on your list, since they will likely have similar jobs. For example, if you are interested in working at an ice cream shop and have Dairy Queen on the list, add competitors such as TCBY.

You should also consider the general level of expertise required for the jobs offered by the businesses you are interested in. Teens searching for an entry-level job might want to add companies that they know have hired other teens, such as retail stores. Those with higher-level skills, who have completed an emergency medical technician (EMT) or welding course, for example, should add companies that require these skills.

> "The YMCA has been involved in my life since I was little."[18]
>
> —Nicolas Cress, YMCA day camp counselor

## Conducting an Internet Search

Once you have a starting list of potential employers, search for each one online to learn more about it and whether it is hiring. Thoroughly review any information about the company that you find on its website. This will allow you to better understand the type of work it does and how you may fit in. Next, check to see whether the website has a career page where you can search available jobs. If it does, make a note of the jobs you are interested in and how to apply. If it does not, make a list of the company's address and contact information; you can then call the company to see whether it has any job openings and inquire what the application process is.

After researching companies already on your list, continue to identify more companies to add to it. The best way to do this is to visit and register on career websites, where companies and organizations post jobs and where prospective employees can post

*Once you start a list of potential employers, research them online to learn more about them and to see whether they are hiring.*

résumés. Job seekers can search for jobs using the site's search engine to enter keywords and locations. Users can even set up a search and have results emailed to them as new jobs are posted. There are multitudes of career websites where one can search for jobs—Monster and Indeed are popular ones. Additionally, there are career search websites that cater to those with less experience, such as Snagajob and Hire Teen.

On these websites, you can create an account profile and upload a résumé. This is important for two reasons—first, it enables companies searching for candidates to find you online, and they may contact you without your even applying for a job. The second reason is that with a résumé uploaded, you can apply for a job right on the website.

Annie registered on the site Snagajob during her online job search, which allowed her to quickly and easily apply for a job she was interested in. Annie is now working at a salad restaurant. "My story is short and sweet, I one click applied to a place that had a name I liked," she explains. "I got a callback the next day, went in for an interview two days later, and was hired by the end of the week. I am still getting callbacks from a couple other places I applied to as well. While I'm happy to have options, I found a job I enjoy."[19]

## In-Person Visits

Although online searching is one way to conduct a job search, the old-fashioned way of visiting places of business to find out whether they are hiring is another fruitful method. Dress nicely, go to the companies on your list, bring copies of your résumé, and ask to speak to a manager. Let the manager know that you are searching for a job and are interested in that company, and

## Search Results Lead to Different Path

As college graduation approached, Aryanto Wijaya of Indonesia began his job search. He set up searches on various career websites seeking a position at a large-scale company, which he believed would result in a higher salary. However, the job postings he received one day included a listing for a website editor for a nonprofit organization. Although Wijaya thought the job sounded interesting, at first he was reluctant to apply because nonprofit organizations generally pay less than for-profit companies. Eventually, however, he applied for the job and was offered it. He was also offered one at a larger company but decided that the nonprofit job was the right one. Months later, reflecting on his experience, Wijaya says he believes he made the right decision. "I used to think that an ideal job was a job that paid well. I thought that a high salary could give me happiness because I could then buy anything I wanted and travel to new places that I haven't visited. But my current job as an editor has changed my perspective," he explains. He is happy to be doing something he considers worthwhile while earning enough to live on his own.

Aryanto Wijaya, "God's Unexpected Plan in My Failed Job-Hunt," YMI, July 17, 2017. https://ymi.today.

ask whether the company is hiring. If the answer is yes, find out whether the company prefers to receive applications online or in person. No matter the answer, give the manager a résumé and thank him or her. This will allow the manager to connect a face to a name when he or she reviews applications.

Statistics show that an in-person visit can increase your chances of getting a job because it will help you stand out among the others applying for the job. A survey called The Multi-Generational Job Search Study, designed by Dan Schawbel, owner of research and consulting firm Millennial Branding, found that only 4 percent of forty-eight- to sixty-seven-year-olds, 5 percent of thirty- to forty-seven-year-olds, and 8 percent of eighteen- to twenty-nine-year-olds spend time job searching offline. "Many people spend so much time online that they forget that the strongest relationships are created offline, face-to-face. People are getting resumes online all the time and as a result, you become a number," says Schawbel. "You have a much better chance of getting your resume to the right person and getting it noticed by facilitating a personal introduction."[20]

> "Many people spend so much time online that they forget that the strongest relationships are created offline, face-to-face."[20]
>
> —Dan Schawbel, owner of a consulting firm

Kinsey Sturgeon discovered this when visiting prospective employers while searching for a summer job. Having previously worked at an ice cream shop, a parking lot, and a movie theater, she knew that she did not want any of those types of jobs. Instead, she decided that a job in retail would interest her because she liked both the idea of dealing with people and getting a discount at the store (a typical perk of retail work). In order to determine where she should apply, Sturgeon took a walk around nearby malls. She recounts:

So, I took to the mall. I started with my favorite stores, obviously—because if I was going to get a discount, I

*Although online job searching is prevalent today, the old-fashioned way of visiting companies in person can be a fruitful method. Dress nicely, bring your résumé, and ask to speak with a manager.*

wanted to use it. Most places told me they weren't hiring or were only hiring for a position that I definitely wasn't qualified for, but a few told me to apply online or handed me an application. I filled out the online applications and turned back in the paper ones and waited.

After a few days, I got a call from Rue21 at the Castleton mall to come in for an interview. I excitedly told them yes. Between then and the interview, I also got a call from Claire's in Noblesville, much closer to home, for an interview. I told them yes as well for the middle of the following week.[21]

Sturgeon interviewed and was hired by Claire's, where she loves her work. Visiting the stores in person played a major role in her obtaining the right job.

## Keep an Open Mind

When researching what jobs to apply for, always keep an open mind. Sometimes you can find an opportunity at a company you never considered, which is what happened to Kai. "At my school, they usually have posters and events and job openings, and what I noticed was FedEx and its benefits," she explains. Although Kai had not considered the company as a potential employer before, she realized that both the pay and the flexible hours would work well for her. So she decided to apply. Kai was called in for an interview and ultimately offered a job as a package handler. Keeping an open mind enabled her to find a new job with good pay.

Kai, "FedEx Ground Package Handler, My First Day," YouTube, August 8, 2017. www.youtube.com/watch?v=hy9Gvp7uh4Y.

## Keeping Track

An important key to a successful job search is to remain organized and methodical. Using a spreadsheet such as those you can create in Excel is one of the best ways to do this. On a spreadsheet, you can list places of business in rows and store information about each one in columns. For example, one column might contain contact information, another might specify whether the company has job openings, and still others might indicate whether you have submitted an application and/or visited the business in person.

As your spreadsheet grows, you will get a good picture of what kind of jobs and companies exist that pique your interest. The more information you have available to you about job opportunities, the better your chances of finding a rewarding, fulfilling job.

# CHAPTER FIVE

# Applying for the Job

You've done it. You've identified businesses that you are interested in working for that have job openings. Now what? How does one successfully apply for a job? The answer depends on whether you are applying for a job online through a company's website or career website or in person at the company or organization.

## Applying Online

Typically, to apply for a job on a company's website, you start by clicking an apply button on the job listing. At this point, you might see a more detailed description of the job and the qualifications required. Review these carefully to make sure that the job still appeals to you and that you meet the qualifications. To continue, you will likely be asked to complete a profile. This will include your contact information and may also include information about your skills, experience, and education. Space is often limited on the application, so focus on skills and characteristics that make you right for the job. For example, Maurice, who applied online for a job at Starbucks, explains, "When you are putting in your resume [for Starbucks], you want to focus on customer service because Starbucks is a customer service based business—that's their main thing."[22] He recommends using keywords from the job description in your application to refer to any relevant skills or experience you possess.

Online applications usually have an area where you can upload your résumé and cover letter. Once you have done this, the last step is to submit your application and log that you have done so in your job search spreadsheet. On this spreadsheet, you can track whether and when you hear back from the company, and any specific notes you want to remember about the company.

The process of applying for jobs on career websites is similar. However, before you apply for a job on a career website like Monster, check the company website to see whether the job posting appears there. If so, it is better to apply directly through the company site than the career website. According to data by Jobs2web, a business that helps firms analyze hiring data, six times as many people apply through job boards as through company websites. Applying directly on the company's website means that you will be competing against fewer people for the job, thereby increasing your chances of obtaining it. If the job is not on the company website, then follow the process on the career website to apply for it.

At this point, you may feel that you have completed the process. However, it will benefit you to then visit the business, if possible, and ask to speak to the manager. Explain that you have applied online and are very interested in the job, and provide him or her with a printed résumé and cover letter. Another option is to call the organization, ask to speak to the manager, and restate your interest in the job. After Kei applied online for the position of beauty advisor at Ulta Beauty, this is exactly what she did. "I think that helps to show that you are really committed and want the job. I personally did this because I really wanted the job,"[23] Kei says. Ultimately, the company called her in for an interview, and she got the position.

> "I think that [calling a store after applying online] helps to show that you are really committed and want the job. I personally did this because I really wanted the job."[23]
>
> —Kei, prestige beauty advisor at Ulta Beauty

## On-Site Job Applications

In some cases companies may have job applications that can be filled out on-site or have both online and on-site applications. If it is an option, applying on-site can give you an edge. This is particularly true at companies or stores that need to fill openings quickly, such as restaurants. "Bartending is the type of job where it makes sense to go in person even if you found out about the opening online," explains Ashley Stahl, career coach. "There is a quick turnaround between the vacancy and the hiring in this industry."[24]

Before you visit a company or organization to apply in person, be sure you are prepared. Have a copy of your résumé and cover letter ready, and take a blue or black pen with which to fill out the application. Dress conservatively to convey a professional impression, and put your mobile phone away. You want to impress the manager by showing that you are serious about the job.

When you arrive at the business, ask for the manager, state your interest in the job opening, and request an application form. Take care to make eye contact and speak clearly and politely.

*Some companies may have job applications that can be filled out both online or on-site. Applying on-site can give you an edge, particularly if an opening needs to be filled quickly.*

## Apply to Many Locations

When you want to work at a retail or restaurant chain, apply to multiple locations if it is feasible to do so. The job market is competitive, and the more applications you submit, the better your chances of being hired. Lauren Somerville, a high school student, recommends applying to every location within a reasonable travel distance because different branches have different managers and staffing needs. "I applied to about 6 Walgreens . . . and the sixth one is the one that called me for an interview," she says.

Lauren Somerville, "How to Get a Job in High School," YouTube, August 29, 2015. www .youtube.com/watch?v=t9VEYP7NLWk.

Use your blue or black pen to complete the application, which typically will ask for the same kind of information as online applications. Refer to your résumé to help you fill out the application, and complete the form as neatly as possible.

Return your completed form to the manager and provide him or her with a résumé or cover letter as well, even if you are not asked to do so. This also demonstrates your seriousness about wanting the job and may give you a professional edge over other applicants. Make sure to thank the manager and offer to quickly provide additional information if any is needed.

## Not Hiring

When visiting companies where you want to apply, you may discover that they are not hiring after all. In this case offer them your résumé and cover letter anyway, because there may be openings in the future. If that happens, having visited in person will give you an edge because the business will have already met you and will have your information on file.

Sam arrived at Sally Hershberger salon in Los Angeles with her résumé in hand. While at cosmetology school, she had toured many salons and was interested in working at this one because the salon's culture matched her personality. She did not know whether the salon was hiring but arrived ready to apply if it was. The manager told her the salon was not currently hiring but might be in the future, so she thanked the manager and left her résumé behind. As she walked out to her car, her phone rang. "It was the manager and she said, hey did you just drop off your resume? And I was like, I did, she's like can you come back up for an interview," Sam says. "So I was like, oh my god, this is the best day ever."[25] Sam went back for an interview and was offered a work trial. This is a common practice in which a prospective employee works for a short time at a job to demonstrate that he or she is qualified and suitable to be hired permanently. Sam ended up working at the salon for four years before opening a salon of her own.

For a person with little to no job experience, the best reference choice would be a coach or teacher. Do not use a person as a reference unless you are sure they will give you a positive review.

# Impress at the Follow-Up

After you apply for a job online or in person, making a follow-up visit can greatly increase your chances of getting the job. For this reason, take steps to make a positive impression. "Dress to impress. Treat this as a job interview," says Kim Costa, job search specialist. "Go in looking polished and professional. You don't want to give the employer a bad impression like if you show up from a work out all stinky," she explains. Costa advises being considerate by visiting during off-peak hours so that you are not inconveniencing anyone who is busy. Costa also recommends that you be prepared for an interview—the manager may decide to interview you on the spot.

Kim Costa, "Following Up on a Job Application," Snagajob. www.snagajob.com.

## References

When applying for a job either online or in person, ensure that you have references ready in case they are requested. References are people who can attest to your previous work in an area, character, and work ethic, as well as provide reasons why you would be a good person to hire. Many companies ask job seekers to provide references on their applications.

When deciding whom to use as references, there are three important factors to consider. First, is the person qualified to provide a reference? Your best friend or an aunt or uncle are not good choices. You want references who are familiar with your work as well as your character. For a person with job experience, the best reference choices are past managers and coworkers. A person with little to no experience would do best to choose a teacher, coach, or adviser at a volunteer activity. The second important factor is to choose someone who will give positive reviews. Do not provide anyone as a reference unless you are sure they will do so. Lastly, ensure that the person knows you are using him or her as a reference. Explain what types of jobs you are applying for so he or she can be ready with relevant examples that demonstrate you would be an excellent employee.

Once you have reached the point of submitting applications and following up with visits, the job search can become quite busy. Be sure to be prepared for emotional ups and downs because the process often includes rejections, no matter how qualified you are. However, if you refuse to let the rejections upset you and stay focused on your goal, your chances of success will be much higher.

# CHAPTER SIX

# You've Got
# an Interview

During an online search, Kevin Young spotted a job that would be perfect for him: YouTube was looking for young people who knew pop culture and could be witty and funny on camera. Young applied and was invited to interview. He expected to do well in the interview—but he didn't. Asked to discuss his favorite meme, he blanked out. He finally mentioned the only one he could think of, but he admits, "[This meme] was one I knew nothing about and I ended up stammering for a couple of seconds."[26] Unable to maintain his composure, he continued to struggle to answer questions that should have been easy for him, and when the interview was over, he even forgot to shake hands with the interviewers. He was not offered the job.

Avoiding an experience like Young's requires being fully prepared for interviews. When a company requests an interview, it means you have passed the first major hurdle. Of all the applicants, the company chose you to actually be considered for the job. The interview is the company's opportunity to get to know you better and see if you will fit well in the job. At the same time, it is also a chance for you to learn more about the job to decide whether it feels right for you. While an interview may sound nerve wracking, it does not need to be if you prepare and practice beforehand.

## Preparation

When you receive a call offering you an interview for a job for which you applied, remain calm and professional no matter how excited you feel. Write down all the information, including the date, time, and place of the interview. The person calling may not be the same person who will interview you, so be sure you know whom the interview is with. Finally, thank the caller and tell him or her that you are looking forward to the interview.

Channel the energy from your excitement into preparing for the interview. First review the information you have compiled about the business so you are familiar with its mission and how it operates. This will allow you to speak knowledgeably about it in person. Then carefully reread the job description to make sure you understand what your potential duties would be.

The next step is to formulate questions an interviewer might ask, such as those involving situations you may encounter on the job. For example, if the job is as a clerk at a bookstore, a possible interview question might be, "What would you do if a customer asks you to find a book and the store does not carry it?" A question for a web developer position might be, "What is your preferred programming language and why?"

> "[This meme] was one I knew nothing about and I ended up stammering for a couple of seconds."[26]
>
> —Kevin Young, discussing a failed interview

Generic interview questions—questions interviewers commonly ask no matter what the job is—are available online and are easily located by searching for the phrase "typical interview questions." Examples include asking applicants to describe their strengths and weaknesses and to talk about what motivates them.

Practice interviewing by enlisting others to ask you all the questions, specific and general, that you have compiled. Lauren, who had already worked in several different jobs by the time she entered college, explains this technique. "So go ahead and grab your mom, grab your brother, sister, . . . a friend, and have them start asking you questions that are typical of interviews," she says. "[Questions] like what are you looking for in this job and why should we hire you."[27]

You may be interviewed by one person, by different people one at a time, or by a group of people. In a group setting, according to interview coach Margaret Buj, "It's very important to be an active contributor and you don't just observe what other people are doing."[28] Being aware of and prepared for these possibilities will ensure that you do not become flustered if the interview is different from what you expected.

An additional preparation strategy is to have a few questions ready to ask the interviewer at the end of the interview. Make sure the questions are thoughtful and pertain to job responsibilities or expectations for employees. This will demonstrate that you are thoughtful and serious about the job. However, career experts

Remain calm and professional when you receive a call offering you an interview for a job. Write down all the information, including the date, time, and place of the interview.

## What Not to Do

There are two major interview don'ts, says Rachel Bitte, chief people officer at a recruiting software company, that will almost immediately doom an applicant's chances of getting the job. The first is failing to treat other people with respect. For example, Bitte set up a lunch interview with a candidate and was appalled at the candidate's rude behavior. "How she treated the wait staff told me something about her as a person," Bitte says. "I just was like, 'Wow.'" The second red flag is failing to ask the interviewer any questions—this implies a lack of curiosity or enthusiasm for the job. Avoid these two behaviors to increase your chances of being hired.

Quoted in Áine Cain, "The 2 Worst Mistakes You Could Make in a Job Interview, According to an Ex-Apple Recruiter," Business Insider, September 6, 2017. www.businessinsider.com.

advise that unless the interviewer brings it up, do not ask questions about pay or benefits. It is better to discuss those topics after you have received an offer.

## Interview Day

The night before the interview, be sure to get a good night's sleep. On the day of the big event, eat enough healthy food beforehand to give you energy. Of course, do not neglect to shower, brush your teeth, and otherwise be as well groomed as possible.

In most cases it is best to dress professionally and conservatively rather than wear a trendy outfit. Depending on the job, though, you may want to dress in the same way as current employees at the business. Kei had observed that Ulta Beauty employees typically wear black outfits. "[For my interview,] I wore black leggings, a sweater, and boots," she recalls. "If you go dressed in black, they may see you more as a potential employee."[29] Kei now works as a premier beauty adviser at Ulta Beauty. Ericka, a high school junior, noticed that employees at

Be as well groomed as possible when you go for an interview. In most cases it is best to dress professionally and conservatively rather than wear a trendy outfit.

the yogurt shop where she applied had to wear their hair up if it was long, so she wore her hair in a bun for her interview. She was offered the job.

Take care to ensure that you arrive at the interview on time or even a few minutes early. Greet your interviewer with a smile and a handshake. Introduce yourself and tell your interviewer that it is nice to meet him or her. At all times, be polite and positive.

When the interview begins, do your best not to be nervous. Your practice interviews will have prepared you for most if not all questions, so allow the awareness that you are ready to answer them bolster your self-confidence. Think positive thoughts. "Turn off your negative self-talk and then create a different self-talk message, like, 'I am here to share to the best of my ability and that is all I can really do,'"[30] says John B. Molidor, coauthor with Barbara Parus of *Crazy Good Interviewing*.

Pay close attention to what the interviewer is asking, and take time to gather your thoughts before answering if you need to.

There is no rush, and interviewers like to see applicants display thoughtfulness. So if you do not understand a question, there is nothing wrong with asking the interviewer to repeat it or clarify it further. Answer questions as succinctly as possible. Most important, be yourself.

Toward the end of the interview, ask the questions about the position that you prepared beforehand when the interviewer prompts you to do so. If your questions have already been answered in the course of the interview, it is fine to say so. Be sure, however, to ask the interviewer what the next steps are in the hiring process and what the time frame is for filling the position, so

## Sardines and Other Unexpected Problems

No matter how much you prepare for an interview, the unexpected may happen. The key is not to let that distract or worry you during the interview. On Glassdoor, a career website, people posted unique situations that they had to deal with during interviews. For one person, it was an intense odor.

> I was a [first] year lawyer and I interviewed at one of the largest, most prestigious firms in my geographic area. Upon arriving and parking my car in the garage, I stepped in an open can of sardines, and spent the next 15 minutes trying to rid my interview shoes (I only wore these heels for interviews) of the sardine smell. Needless to say, as nervous as I was about the stench, I managed to toughen it up, nail the interview, and get the job offer.

Keeping your focus and poise in an awkward situation might actually help you get the job because it shows the employer that you are confident and able to cope with an unexpected setback.

Quoted in Emily Moore, "5 Interview Stories That Will Make You Cringe," Glassdoor, March 23, 2017. www.glassdoor.com.

that you have an idea when you might expect to be contacted. At the conclusion of the interview, again shake the interviewer's hand, make eye contact, and thank him or her for considering you.

## Follow Up

As with submitting a job application, your work is not finished when the interview is over. Take action to increase your likelihood of receiving a job offer and/or being called back for a second interview. First, write a summary of the interview. List the questions that you were asked, the questions that you asked, and the answers to both. This could be helpful if you are invited to a second interview. Then, within 24 hours after the interview, write a thank-you note, either on paper or via email, to every person who interviewed you. Keep the note simple—thank the person for meeting with you, reiterate your interest in the job, and state that you look forward to hearing from him or her.

At this point, the waiting begins—but you should keep busy researching other potential employers, applying for other jobs, and networking. Not only will this keep you from fretting about the interview results, it will also continue to open up new possibilities. Eventually, your efforts will pay off, as long as you remain patient and persistent.

# CHAPTER SEVEN

# The Job
# Is Yours

As her nursing school graduation approached, Krystal Dantzler began applying for hospital staff positions. She had little work history as a nurse and knew she was competing with applicants who did, including her classmates who had worked as certified nursing assistants. But she continued to apply to hospital after hospital, until she finally landed an interview. Four days later, she was singing at church choir practice when her phone rang. It was the recruiter from the hospital. "[The recruiter said,] 'One of the ladies who interviewed you loved you and wants to offer you a position.' When she said those words, I don't know how to explain it, I literally started to get so emotional [because] I worked so hard for something and it came full circle,"[31] Dantzler explains. She accepted the position as a registered nurse and more than a year later is still enthusiastic about her job.

Most people receive job offers over the phone as Dantzler did, although offers may also be made through email or even in person immediately after an interview. The time period between an interview and an offer can vary greatly, depending on the hiring company. As exciting as it is to receive a job offer, it is best to get specific details and information before deciding whether to accept the job.

## The Details

If you are offered a job, typically you do not want to accept immediately unless you are sure it is your dream job and all aspects of it are acceptable to you. In most cases, though, as Alison Doyle, a job search expert with Balance Careers, recommends, "Be sure to emphasize your gratitude and your interest in the job, and then ask if there is a deadline by which you have to make your decision. If you think you need more time than they give you, it is okay to ask for a bit more time. However, do not put off the decision for so long that they rescind your offer."[32]

Before making your decision, there are many things you need to find out. These include the start date, salary, hours, benefits such as health insurance and vacation and sick days, and who your supervisor will be. An additional consideration is whether your personality and skills will be a good fit within the company's culture. Only after evaluating all of these should you decide whether to accept, reject, or negotiate the offer. Negotiation is more common with higher-level jobs at businesses that have some flexibility regarding wages and benefits.

Often it helps to discuss the offer with close family members, especially those in the work force, to gather their thoughts. Discuss the pros and cons of the offer, and job itself, then consider all of these. Once you have made a decision, contact the person who offered you the job. Begin by again thanking him or her for the offer, then accept, decline, or state that you are interested but wish to know whether any aspects of the offer are negotiable.

> "I literally started to get so emotional [because] I worked so hard for something and it came full circle."[31]
>
> —Krystal Dantzler, on receiving a job offer

## Negotiating an Offer

To negotiate successfully for a better offer, it is imperative that you are well prepared. "There are a number of steps you can take to negotiate effectively," recommends Doyle. "First, research salaries for the job to get a sense of what you're worth. Think about

## Job Perks

Some jobs offer perks that go beyond salary and benefits. For example, employees at a clothing store may get a discount on anything they buy at the store, while restaurant workers may receive food discounts or even free meals. In Rachel Denison's case, enjoying a pool during off hours was an advantage of being a lifeguard. "Pool memberships are not cheap these days," Denison writes. "Being a lifeguard provided me with free access to a pool whenever I wanted to relax, sunbathe or swim. If I got sweaty being in the sun, I would just take a quick dip in the pool. Shifts on the stand are usually only 15 to 20 minutes long, so relief was never far away."

Rachel Denison, "6 Reasons Lifeguarding Is the Best Job Ever," Snagajob. www.snagajob .com.

what combination of salary and benefits would work for you—this will be your counter offer."[33]

Use the research you have performed to support your counteroffer. Provide statistics regarding comparable salaries in the same type of job for someone with your experience. In response, the company may then counter with another offer that is more than its original one but less than your counteroffer. You can accept that offer or continue to try to negotiate—but have reasonable expectations. When Valerie was offered a job in the education field, she decided to negotiate the salary. "Valerie, who works in higher education, received an offer for 50K [$50,000], fair for her role and experience in the field," says an article by the Muse. "Still, she wasn't going to not negotiate, and she asked if they could go up five thousand more. They couldn't quite go there,

If a job is offered to you, don't accept it immediately unless you are sure it is your dream job. Instead, express gratitude for the offer and ask for a little time to make your decision.

so in the end, she signed on at 52K [$52,000]. What's more: She was able to get a relocation bonus for $2,000, an unusual benefit in that industry."[34]

## First-Day Experiences

Once a person has accepted an offer and agreed to a start date, it is time to get to work. On your first day, show up on time and with a positive, flexible attitude as the first time can be chaotic. Maia McCormick remembers the early days of working as a software developer at Spring. He describes the time as a confusion of meeting people, being assigned a work space, and setting up the development environment on his computer.

Thinking back on it now, that first day was a blur of new people, computer set-up nonsense, and free snacks (snacks which continue to be an integral part of my Spring experience).

Anyone who's set up a dev environment recently knows it takes about 20 times longer than you think it should, no matter how good the onboarding guide is (and Spring's is pretty comprehensive). My first two days were spent installing software, transferring over dotfiles, and getting our app to build on my machine.[35]

Like McCormick, most people face an onslaught of new information and people during the first days of work. A new job usually begins with some form of training that can last for several days or even weeks, depending on the complexity of the job. The training may be formal, like classes for new employees, or informal, such as a new employee shadowing an experienced one as he or she

## Getting Paid

On your first day at a new job, you will fill out many forms, including a W-4, which lets your employer know how much tax to deduct from your pay. Typically, you will also fill out a form indicating whether you want to receive your pay via direct deposit, in which your paycheck is electronically deposited into your bank account, or a paper check that you can either deposit or cash. Every pay period, you will receive a paper or electronic pay stub. The pay stub will show your gross pay, which is the amount you earned before taxes are taken out. It also shows health insurance premiums and any money you allocate to a retirement fund, such as a 401K, which are deducted from your pay. The pay stub also displays your net pay, the amount that you receive after all of these deductions are taken out. Being aware of your net pay amount is essential for you to plan a budget that will enable you to spend and save your wages wisely.

performs work duties. Rosemics Campbell was hired by T.J.Maxx to work on the floor sorting clothes and scanning items. Her first day began with training. "Because this is the first day, they taught me the machine that I will use because I'm on the floor scanning the price tags. They taught me how to scan . . . and I needed to sort the dresses from small, medium to large,"[36] she explains. She was then put to work on her own and at first was discouraged as she continually received errors on the scanning machine. By the end of the day, however, Campbell had mastered the machine and completed her assigned tasks on time.

## Strategies for Success

The first weeks of a new job can be extremely overwhelming because there is so much to learn. A new employee must acquire new skills and learn how to deal with unfamiliar situations and challenges. However, keep in mind that new employees are not expected to know everything at first, so use this time to grow your knowledge as quickly as possible.

The first weeks of a new job can be overwhelming because there is so much to learn. Listen carefully as you are being trained and do not hesitate to ask questions if something is not clear.

Listen carefully as you are being trained, and do not hesitate to ask questions about anything you do not understand. Take notes either on the job or at the end of the day so you have them to refer to if you forget how to do something you were trained on.

Attempt to quickly memorize the names of your colleagues and bosses, and greet them each day. Take time to get to know the people you are working with and establish good relationships with them. Doing so will give them a favorable impression of you, and make working more pleasant. Maintain a positive attitude, and never pass up an opportunity to offer help to a manager or coworker, even if the task is something outside of your job description like unpacking and storing a delivery of office supplies. Above all, steer clear of office gossip. "The workplace can be full of rumors and gossip. Your mission should be to stay above the fray," writes Angela Copeland, career coach. "Avoid the office gossips and don't get involved in any office trash talk or politics, especially on your first day at work."[37]

> "The workplace can be full of rumors and gossip. Your mission should be to stay above the fray."[37]
>
> —Angela Copeland, career coach

As challenging as it may seem at first, you will soon be comfortable in your new job and reaping the benefits of working. Always do the best you can and be the best person you can be at work. Whether you stay at this job or try to obtain a new one, performing well and displaying good character will yield benefits such as promotions, raises, and the satisfaction of doing a job well.

# SOURCE NOTES

## Introduction: Different Jobs at Different Stages

1. Quoted in Quora, "Why Did You Get a Job as a Teenager?," April 17, 2017. www.quora.com.
2. Quoted in Anthony O'Neil, "What to Expect at Your First Job," YouTube, May 17, 2017. www.youtube.com/watch?v=8hMD-Lgyz5l.
3. Vicki Salemi, "How to Ride the Emotions of Your First Job Search," Monster, 2018. www.monster.com.

## Chapter One: What Kind of Work Should I Do?

4. Quoted in Arielle Pardes, "Why Your First Job Out of College Always Sucks," *Vice*, June 17, 2016. www.vice.com.
5. Alyssa, "About Me," Human Training by Alyssa, 2018. https://humanetrainingbyalyssa.com.
6. Quoted in Muse Editor, "How I Landed a Job That Matched My Skills and Interests Perfectly," Muse, 2019. www.themuse.com.

## Chapter Two: Résumé Rules

7. Ben Talks, "How to Become a Web Developer Without a Degree," YouTube, April 27, 2017. www.youtube.com/watch?v=zKaXtUXrOtY.
8. Quoted in Victoria C., "Seven Things to Know Before Writing Your First Resume," Experience, January 29, 2017. www.experience.com.
9. Quoted in Lauren Settembrino, "Caught in a Resume Lie: The Stories of Fibbing Job Seekers," TopResume, 2019. www.topresume.com.
10. Quoted in Catherine Conlan, "More Adjectives Every Resume Should Include," Monster, 2018. www.monster.com.
11. Quoted in Elmbrook Schools, "Alumni Spotlight—Leslie Kirchoff," March 3, 2017. www.elmbrookschools.org.

## Chapter Three: Networking

12. Quoted in Quora, "Have You Ever Gotten a Job Purely Through Networking?," August 23, 2014. www.quora.com.
13. David Carlson, "How I Networked into Almost Every Job I've Ever Had," Young Adult Money, July 7, 2014. www.youngadultmoney.com.
14. Kristen McCabe, "9 Networking Tips for Real People from a Real (Awkward) Girl," G2 Crowd, April 13, 2018. https://learn.g2crowd.com.
15. Mario Wilson, "If You Attend Networking Meetings, These 6 Tips Will Help You Perfect Your 30 Second Commercial," LinkedIn, September 6, 2016. www.linkedin.com.
16. Moriah Rahamim, "How I Got 7 Job Offers in 8 Weeks," *Noteworthy* (blog), July 9, 2018. https://blog.usejournal.com.
17. Quoted in Elizabeth Mack, "7 Social Media Habits That Disqualified Candidates, According to Hiring Managers," Ladders, March 12, 2018. www.theladders.com.

## Chapter Four: The Search

18. Nicolas Cress, "My Life at the YMCA!," *Y Blog*, YMCA Spokane, June 14, 2012. http://blog.ymcaspokane.org.
19. Quoted in Kim Costa, "How Annie Nailed Her Interview and Got Hired," Snagajob. www.snagajob.com.
20. Quoted in Eric Bloom, "Job Search the Old Fashioned Way; It's Harder, but It Works," ITworld, October 29, 2012. www.itworld.com.
21. Kinsey Sturgeon, "How I Fell in Love Working at Claire's," Odyssey, May 8, 2017. www.theodysseyonline.com.

## Chapter Five: Applying for the Job

22. Maurice W., "How to Get Hired at Starbucks—Get a Job at Starbucks Fast!," YouTube, June 4, 2017. www.youtube.com/watch?v=nLPAxVIZZKE.
23. Kei, "How to Get a Job at Ulta Beauty," YouTube, June 10, 2017. www.youtube.com/watch?v=lv-vAX8EVPI.

24. Ashley Stahl, "Should You Apply for Jobs Online or in Person?," *Forbes*, July 13, 2017. www.forbes.com.
25. Sam, "How I Got My Job, and Where I'm Going," Khan Academy, 2017. www.khanacademy.org.

## Chapter Six: You've Got an Interview

26. Kevin Young, "Millennial Job Interview Fail," YouTube, October 26, 2015. www.youtube.com/watch?v=XZ-Ou2Mf5O8.
27. Lauren, "Getting a Job as a Teenager," YouTube, August 2, 2015. www.youtube.com/watch?v=gTW19pZ2kdQ.
28. Quoted in FV1 Magazine, "How to Shine in a Group Interview," October 12, 2012. www.youtube.com/watch?v=BgoX w084K88.
29. Kei, "How to Get a Job at Ulta Beauty."
30. Quoted in Amy Levin-Epstein, "5 Ways to Look Relaxed During a Job Interview," CBS News, March 26, 2013. www.cbs news.com.

## Chapter Seven: The Job Is Yours

31. Krystal Dantzler, "I Got the Job—Job Offer Story," YouTube, April 14, 2018. www.youtube.com/watch?v=wjbxowQj8uY.
32. Alison Doyle, "How to Negotiate, Accept or Decline a Job Offer," Balance Careers, November 2, 2018. www.thebalance careers.com.
33. Doyle, "How to Negotiate, Accept or Decline a Job Offer."
34. Muse, "8 Real People Share Their Successful Negotiation Stories," *Forbes*, August 8, 2017. www.forbes.com.
35. Maia McCormick, "28 Days Later: My First Four Weeks as a Junior Engineer at Spring," *Maia McCormick* (blog), June 16, 2015. http://code.maiamccormick.com.
36. Rosemics Campbell, "My First Day at TJ Maxx," YouTube, April 26, 2018. www.youtube.com/watch?v=n5Oaue0YQVA.
37. Angela Copeland, "9 Tips for Making a Great Impression at Your New Job," LiveCareer, www.livecareer.com.

# FOR MORE INFORMATION

## Books

Carol Christen and Richard Bolles, *What Color Is Your Parachute for Teens*. Berkeley, CA: Ten Speed, 2015.

Laura DeCarlo, *Résumés for Dummies*. Foster City, CA: For Dummies, 2019.

Ivan Misner and Brian Hilliard, *Networking Like a Pro: Turning Contacts into Connections*. Irvine, CA: Entrepreneur, 2017.

Angela Rose, *LinkedIn in 30 Minutes: How to Create a Rock-Solid LinkedIn Profile and Build Connections That Matter*. 2nd ed. Boston: In 30 Minutes, 2016.

Robin Ryan, *60 Seconds and You're Hired!* Rev. ed. New York: Penguin, 2016.

## Internet Sources

Anna Cooperberg, "The One Career Trick You Need to Learn: Networking," *Teen Vogue*, June 28, 2013. www.teenvogue.com.

Alison Doyle, "Good Job Ideas for Teens," Balance Careers, October 29, 2018. www.thebalancecareers.com.

Princeton Review, "Career Quiz," 2019. www.princetonreview.com.

Molly Thompson, "How Teens Can Find a Job," Chron, 2019. https://work.chron.com.

## Websites

**LinkedIn** (www.linkedin.com). On this website, users can search for jobs, post a résumé and profile, and connect with others. Additionally, users can join groups on this website to meet others with similar career interests.

**Resume.com** (www.resume.com). This website provides free templates to create résumés.

**Snagajob** (www.snagajob.com). This career website is a job search site for hourly paid jobs, with more than three hundred thousand employer locations. People can search the website for jobs and post a résumé and profile. Additionally, there are articles about career searches and how to conduct them.

## Apps

### Good&Co: Culture Fit Jobs

This app provides a personality test that allows users to discover strengths and matches to companies that seek employees with those strengths. This is for job seekers of all different levels of experience.

### Resume: CV Builder and Designer for Your Job

This app allows users to use one of the twenty résumé templates to create résumés or a curriculum vitae (CV). Users can then export the résumé they create as a PDF.

### ZipRecruiter Job Search

This app allows people to search for jobs using keywords and location. It allows users to be notified if jobs are posted that meet the user's specification.

# INDEX

Note: Boldface page numbers indicate illustrations.